Quick & Easy Tarot
by
Lily Oak

Quick & Easy Tarot
ISBN 978-1-9079-6315-5

Published by
Hedge Witchery Books
www.hedge-witcherybooks.com

Dedication

For Jenson & Scarlet. My two greatest blessings... who I never can predict.

Introduction

Although tarot is now one of the most popular means of divination, it's origins have nothing to do with providing insight or predicting the future.

The tarot deck started life as a card game called "trionfi", the first records of this game date back to mid 15th century Europe. Although there is evidence to suggest that card games may have been used to divine the future from the 16th century, the first kinds of readings we would recognise as a rudimentary tarot spread date from the 18th century, well over 300 year since the cards came into being.

Tarot decks as we use them today consist of the Major Arcana and the Minor Arcana. The Major Arcana contains 22 cards that represent different elements of the human experience of life, the factors that affect it and the responses that can be solicited from it. The Minor Arcana comprises of four suits each representing a different element of our day-to-day lives, each of these suits is made up of fourteen cards that give guidance on that particular aspect of life.

This book is designed to help you learn to use the tarot cards, in as simple and straight forward a way as possible. By the end of this book you will be able to perform tarot readings for yourself and friends. You will also, I hope, have started a life long love affair with the art of tarot, the clarity it can bring and the joy of the ongoing path of learning that this little book provides the first steps along.

How to choose your deck

One of the first things you need in order to start learning to read tarot, is a tarot deck. There are now hundreds of different decks on the market, in wide ranging designs. The one hard and fast rule when buying a tarot deck is: Make sure you are buying a "tarot" deck. I know this sounds like I'm stating the obvious, but bear with me.

As well as there being hundreds of different tarot decks on the market, there are also lots of "oracle" decks. Oracle decks are a great method of divination, but not particularly helpful when trying to learn tarot. The best way to check you are buying a tarot deck, is to look at the number of cards. A full tarot deck should have 78 cards, 22 Major Arcana & 56 Minor Arcana.

Beyond making sure your deck is a tarot deck, there aren't really any other hard and fast rules to stick to. Simply make sure you pick a deck with imagery you connect to. "But how do I know what imagery I 'connect' with?" I hear you ask. Well basically pick a deck you like the look of, one with illustrations you find attractive. Usually it's the one whilst browsing a big display of them you instinctively pick up. The imagery in a deck is what you use to intuitively pick out meanings of cards within readings, so it's important to pick one you will enjoy gazing at.

If you get really stuck when picking a deck, I'd recommend going for one of the traditional ones. Pretty much every modern deck is based, however loosely, on one of the old school decks, so learning with one of these first will stand you in pretty good stead to learn other decks in the future.

"The World", Tarot de Marseille, Jean Dodal, early 18th century.

Connecting with your deck

If you read other books, articles and websites about tarot reading, they will often mention the importance of "connecting" with your deck, or "attuning" to your deck. You may well be wondering what on earth they are talking about, and if it really is as important as is made out. Well, yes, it is quite important, but don't panic, I'll talk you through it.

Connecting with your deck is basically a process of figuring out what the meaning of each card is, for you personally as a reader.

It's true each card has a standard meaning, but this isn't the only thing you use to give a reading. Everyone that picks up any given tarot deck will ascribe slightly different meanings to the cards. To find out what your meaning for the cards are, look at them each in turn and note what it is about the imagery that stands out for you. Once you know the detail that is calling out to you, ask yourself what attributes and associations that particular thing holds for you.

For example, on one of my decks, the Magician is standing in a field of new seedlings. To me the seedlings really stood out, even though they were a very small detail. I associate seedlings with new life, renewal and Spring time. This means for me the Magician card will have these meanings, as well as the standard meanings.

Every time I buy a new deck I take a note pad or sheet of paper and jot down my personal meanings of each card - (as shown on the next page) - and have this in front of me for the first dozen or so readings I do with that particular deck.

0 - Fool - Potential, new beginnings / Foolishness, lack of thought/planning
1 - Magician - Progress, confidence / don't hesitate, "head-in-sand"
2 - High Priestess - A female, secret or answer revealed / over emotional, irrational
3 - Empress - Stability, growth, creativity / Domestic/Career difficulties
4 - Emperor - Success, power, strength of will / warns against weakness or submission
5 - High Priest - Wisdom, insightfulness, understanding, a teacher / lies, misleading advice
6 - Lovers - good relationship, marriage / bad decision, relationship troubles.
7 - Chariot - travel, achievement, goal or stage reached / don't get ruthless or too headstrong
8 - Justice - a need for balance and common sense, you may be judged / Injustice, unfair treatment
9 - Hermit - need to re-evaluate and take stock, a need for introverted judgement / refusal to take advice
10 - Wheel of Fortune - New beginning & change, luck & things working out / bad luck, unfortunate change, or stop & think.
11 - Strength - need courage in face of difficulties, self belief / faltering when faced with obstacles
12 - Hanged Man - Sacrifice & risk leading to happiness / Materialism leading to ill fortune
13 - Death - Development, rebirth, new understanding / destruction
14 - Temperance - Balance, navigating complexities to make things work / lack of harmony
15 - Devil - Harnessing "negative" traits for good / impulsiveness, lack of accountability
16 - Tower - Understanding gained from disaster, rebuilding / ruin brought on yourself
17 - Star - Good luck after some misfortune, new beginning/solution / don't be blind to a new opportunity
18 - Moon - Trust intuition & do not rely on 'logic' too much / "settling" due to over rationalising.
19 - Sun - Triumph & reward, often following hardship or long work / Failure, false success.
20 - Judgement - achievement of goals/inner development, serenity + new beginnings / regret & recriminations
21 - World - Completion & fulfilment / failure, bleak immobility, inability to progress to next level.

CUPS		SWORDS
① Fertility, love, abundance ② - love, friendship, good partner ③ - Happiness & joy from love ④ - Emotional joy (beware too much) ⑤ - good time gone bad, loss, re-assessment ⑥ - Happy memories, the past re-awakened ⑦ - Ambition & Hope ⑧ - Disappointment, need new plan ⑨ - Peace, contentment, fulfilment ⑩ - Peace again, happiness, achievement ⑪ (Knave) - Thoughtful, helpful youth ⑫ (Knight) - Bright, happy youth, a lover ⑬ (Queen) fair, loving, creative women ⑭ (King) Intelligent, successful, worldly man.		①- Success, achievement ② - Good from adversity ③ - Battles clearing, new opportunity ④ - Calm, respite from troubles ⑤ - Struggle, defeat ⑥ - difficulty overcome, travel, good news ⑦ - Obstacles, be brave/careful ⑧ - Obstacles - be patient ⑨ - Failure, be steadfast ⑩ - Disaster, the darkest before the dawn ⑪ (Knave) - Clever young man ⑫ (Knight) - Soldier, a dark strong youth ⑬ (Queen) - Dark clever woman, a widow ⑭ (King) - Dark authoritative man.

PENTACLES		WANDS
①- Material prosperity ② - Disruption to material things ③ - Achievement in career/study ④ - Wealth, highly successful ⑤ - Ruin, financial disaster ⑥ - Financial help, stability ⑦ - material success but tread carefully ⑧ - Rewards for care & work ⑨ - Wealth, achievement ⑩ - Wealth, inherited or given ⑪ (Knave) - a careful, sensible youth ⑫ (Knight) - Honorable young man ⑬ (Queen) - sensible, generous women ⑭ (King) - Careful, practical, successful man.		①- Inspiration, new beginnings ② - Deserved good luck ③ - Gains from brave choices ④ - Success, popularity ⑤ - Setbacks, determination needed ⑥ - Achievement, encouragement ⑦ - Obstacles, but good prospects ⑧ - Progress, be confident ⑨ - Opposition, hold your ground ⑩ - Struggles ⑪ (Knave) - Dark, lively youth, an employee ⑫ (Knight) - Dark, energetic man, a journey ⑬ (Queen) - Practical, dominant woman ⑭ (King) - Powerful, determined man.

The Major Arcana

The Fool is childlike, full of hope and new beginnings,
just hope he doesn't rush to quickly into the new world he's found in.

The Magician is confident, and takes steps that are bold,
just hope he doesn't hesitate or hide from what unfolds.

The Priestess a woman, who can reveal and provide insight,
just hope she doesn't bring emotions so strong rationale is lost from sight.

The Empress is growth, creativity and stability,
just hope she brings not love, family or career difficulty.

The Emperor is success, power and force of will,
just hope he doesn't bring weakness or submission, worse still.

The Priest is understanding, and teachings given,
just hope he does bring deceit or to bad advise you listen.

The Lovers are partnership, truth and friends,
just hope they don't bring disputes and bad decisions in the end.

The Chariot is achievement, goals reached and travel,
just hope it isn't so head-strong it puts you at the ruthless level.

Justice is balance, commons sense rules here,
just hope it treats you justly and not makes the world unfair.

The Hermit re-evaluates, takes time to look within,
just hope he doesn't hear wise words but fail to take them in.

The Wheel is new beginnings, it is luck and it is change,
just hope the luck isn't bad or circumstance poorly arranged.

Strength is courage, pure self belief,
just hope it doesn't flee you in the face of grief.

The Hanged Man is sacrifice, but he leads to happiness,
just be careful being greedy doesn't lead you to distress.

*Death is re-birth, new understanding,
just hope it doesn't lead to destruction when you find him.*

*Temperance is balance, making things work,
just hope it isn't also where lack of harmony lurks.*

*The Devil takes the bad, and turns it to a positive,
just make sure you aren't impulsive and good accounts you can give.*

*The Tower is learning, from things having to be re-built,
just make sure it falling down isn't justly your guilt.*

*The Star is needed luck, an opportunity for you,
just be careful you don't miss out on promising ventures new.*

*The Moon is a psychic, pure intuition,
just don't over rationalise into an unfulfilling position.*

*The Sun is triumph, brought by your own hand,
just hope that it's built on something firmer than sand.*

*Judgement is serenity, happiness in achievement,
just hope the past doesn't linger to spoil this found contentment.*

*The World is completeness, full of fulfilment,
just hope it doesn't hamper progression or bring failure and
disappointment.*

The Major Arcana portion of your deck is comprised of 22 cards which related to life experiences and phases of the human life experience in general.

Everyone in life starts their journey as the "Fool", inexperienced, full of potential, but very naïve and lacking in experience. They will all end it having built their "World" and ready to take the step into the realm beyond our mortal one. Of course they will encounter many people and situations along the way, as are embodied through the other cards in the Major Arcana.

The Major Arcana does not only represent a life experience as one all encompassing journey, but can also represent the hundreds of little undertakings that make up our lives. For example, starting a new career, starting a new relationship, and dealing with changes within a family situation, may all present you with the situations expressed in these cards as well.

Over the next couple of pages you will find the generally accepted meanings of these cards. After reading these I would advise you sit with your deck and take some time connecting with these cards and working out how these meanings translate to you and your deck. I would advise making notes on a large sheet of paper or in a note book, as shown in the "Connecting with your deck" section of this book.

Once you are comfortable with the Major Arcana card meanings you can put these to use and practice using them in readings by doing single card readings and the three card tarot spreads as detailed in the "Readings" section of this book.

Card Meanings

0. "The Fool"
   Right way up: Potential and new beginnings.
   Inverted: Foolishness and a lack of thought or planning.

1. "The Magician"
   Right way up: Progress and confidence.
   Inverted: Hesitation and running away from problems.

2. "The High Priestess"
   Right way up: A woman or female energy, or a secret or answer being revealed.
   Inverted: High emotions and irrational behaviour.

3. "The Empress"
   Right way up: Stability, growth and creativity.
   Inverted: Domestic or career difficulties.

4. "The Emperor"
   Right way up: Success, power and strength of will.
   Inverted: Weakness and submission.

5. "The High Priest"
   Right way up: Wisdom, insight, understanding or a teacher.
   Inverted: Lies and misleading advice.

6. "The Lovers"
   Right way up: Partnership, relationship progressing
   Inverted: Bad decision or relationship problems

7. "The Chariot"
   Right way up: Achievement, a goal reached or travel
   Inverted: Ruthlessness

8. "Justice"
   Right way up: Balance, common sense or that you will be judged
   Inverted: Injustice or unfair treatment

9. "The Hermit"

Right way up: Re-evaluation, "taking stock" of a situation, introspection
Inverted: Refusal to take advice or rushing a decision

10. "The Wheel of Fortune"
Right way up: Situations changing and resolving
Introverted: Unfortunate changes

11. "Strength"
Right way up: Courage in the face of difficulties and self belief
Introverted: Failing in the face of obstacles

12. "The Hanged Man"
Right way up: Sacrifice or taking a worthwhile risk
Inverted: Greed or selfishness leading to misfortune

13. "Death"
Right way up: New understanding, development and re-birth
Inverted: Destruction

14: "Temperance"
Right way up: Balance, finding a solution to complex issues
Inverted: Lack of harmony

15: "The Devil"
Right way up: Turning the bad into the good
Inverted: Impulsiveness or lack of responsibility

16: "The Tower"
Right way up: Rebuilding, gaining knowledge from things gone wrong
Inverted: Ruin brought upon yourself

17: "The Star"
Right way up: Timely god luck or a new solution
Inverted: Missing an opportunity

18: "The Moon"
Right way up: Intuition and trust in your feelings
Inverted: Over rationalising

19: "The Sun"
Right way up: Triumph, reward for hard work and dedication
Inverted: False success or failure

20: "Judgement"
Right way up: Achievement of goals bringing self-development, serenity and new beginnings
Inverted: Regret or recriminations

21: "The World"
Right way up: Completion and fulfilment
Inverted: Inability to progress

Minor Arcana

Cups is the emotion, the joy and the cares,
it's both our elation, and our fears.

1 of cups, is abundance and gain,
2 of cups, the joy of another's name.

3 of cups is joy and happiness,
4 of cups says beware, of it in excess.

5 of cups re-assess, after the good gone bad,
6 of cups the past, may be, re-had.

7 of cups speak of ambition and hope,
8 of cups is disappointment, but widen your scope.

9 of cups is about, peace and contentment,
10 of cups is all that but with added achievement.

The Knave of cups is helpful, the Knight a lover and bright,
The Queen of cups creative and the King brings insight.

Swords are actions, often needed the most,
they slay our demons and, chase our ghosts.

1 of swords, is about achievement and success,
2 of swords gain, from having much less.

3 of swords, a door opens, paths are clear,
4 of swords a rest, from what you fear.

5 of swords shows struggle, and defeat,
6 of swords sees you, back on your feet.

7 of swords show hurdles, be brave and careful,
8 of swords patiences over comes what you thought fretful.

9 of swords failure, be steadfast,
10 of swords disaster, but it will end at last.

The Knave of swords is often clever, the Knight is strong like a soldier,
The Queen of swords quick witted, and the King brings order.

Coins are what we do on this earth,
our house, our home, what's in our purse.

1 of coins is prosperity, to have and hold,
2 of coins says a disruption may unfold.

3 of coins brings achievement in the intellectual
4 of coins show wealth, says we'll be successful.

5 of coins, is financial disaster and ruin,
6 of coins is help, something to stand firm in.

7 of coins success, but please be careful,
8 of coins, hard work will see you successful.

9 of coins is wealth and achievement driven,
10 of coins says there will be a gift you're given.

The Knave of coins is sensible, the Knight is just and true,
the Queen on coins is generous, the King advises to you.

Wands is the need to change, it is our passions,
bringing our ideas into worldly fashions.

1 of wands is inspiration, sees something new begin,
2 of wands sees good luck finally come in.

3 of wands success from being brave,
4 of wands success, and the popularity craved.

5 of wands says there may be, a set-back,
6 of wands gives encouragement, gets your will back.

7 of wands shows things aren't as bad as they seem,
8 of wands sees you closer to your dreams.

9 of wands be strong ,and hold your ground,
10 of wands, struggles may make you frown.

*The Knave of wands is lively, the Knight energy beckons,
the Queen is practical, the King a force to be reckoned.*

The Suits

Cups:

Cups is the suit that deals with matters of the heart. It is linked to the element of water and has links to emotions, as well as imagination and creativity. They also represent spirituality, and the season of Summer.

Swords:

Swords is the suit dealing with intellect. It is linked to the element of air and has links to ideas, plans and learning. They also represent conflict and worries. It often marks the instigation of something, and represents the season of Winter.

Coins:

Coins is the suit that deals with practical and material matters. It is linked to the element of earth and links to money, property and career. They also represent fertility, and the season of Autumn.

Wands:

Wands is the suit dealing with energy and transformation. It is linked to the element of fire and links to changes of circumstance, personal transformations and new beginnings. They also represent communication, and the season of Spring.

The Numbers

Number	Meaning	Inverted Meaning
1	New beginnings	Failure to get new project started or being "stuck"
2	Duality, partnership and balance	Lack of balance
3	Completion of task or an achievement	Facing first hurdle in a task
4	Solid foundations	Poor planning
5	Need to address lack of balance, potential problems	Problems going unchecked and disaster
6	A goal reaching a significant way point	Difficulties that need to be overcome
7	Spiritual and emotional happiness	Contemplation is needed
8	Progress in long running situations	Disappointment and obstacles
9	"Light at the end of the tunnel" and projects nearing completion	Failure to achieve objectives the way you planned
10	Completion, achievement and being ready to move on	Endings and having to start again
Knave	A young person or news	Unfinished projects
Knight	A peer (friend) or bravery and achievement	A peer (unfriendly) cowardice
Queen	A woman or a teacher	Bad advice
King	A man or understanding	Over confidence

Readings

Now you are comfortable with your deck and the card meanings you will no doubt be looking forward to putting them to good use and actually doing some readings.

In order to complete a good reading, preparation is essential. First of all decide when and where you are going to do the reading. You want to be relaxed, comfortable and free from distractions. Make sure you are in a quiet environment wherever possible. Unplug phones, switch mobiles on the silent mode and if there is a busy family rushing round, hang a "do not disturb" sign on the door.

It is also important to be in the right frame of mind to complete a reading. Do not try and do readings if you are stressed or upset. If you've had a busy day at work, don't rush through the front door and grab your tarot deck. Sit down, have some tea and quietly relax for a little while first. I would also strongly advise staying away from high amounts of caffeine, alcohol and other stimulants before attempting a reading.

One of the quickest and simplest ways to start using your cards is to do single cards readings. This involves concentrating one a question whilst shuffling your deck. Cutting the deck and then reading the card that is presented on top of where you made the cut. When doing single card readings I would recommend using just the Major Arcana cards. Doing single card readings is also a very good learning device to acquaint yourself with the Major Arcana cards.

Tarot spreads are the order and patterns we use to lay out the cards. When choosing which spread to use it is important to consider two factors. What information you wish to get from the reading, and how much detail you want from the reading.

Many readers develop their own little rituals for shuffling and cutting the cards. My personal recommendation is to shuffle the deck 3 times then cut in to 3 piles, repeat this until you feel ready to start. If I am reading for another person, I will also ask them to shuffle the cards.

In the tarot spreads illustrated below you will see not only the positions the cards should be placed in, but also the order in which they should be dealt. Start with "1", then "2", etc.

It is customary not to turn any of the cards over until they have all been dealt. They are turned over by lifting the bottom of the card and flipping it upwards, away from the reader.

As with all things in tarot reading follow your instincts, it won't be long before you find yourself wanting to tweak layouts and shuffling styles. This should be considered a good thing as it shows how comfortable you are getting with your cards.

You will also start to notice that in each reading you complete a different detail in the card and it's meaning will seem to stand out for you, just as it did when you went through the process of connecting with your deck. This is natural psychic development and by following your intuition your readings will gain in insight and detail.

3 Card Spreads

Three card spreads can be completed with either a full deck, or just using the Major Arcana.

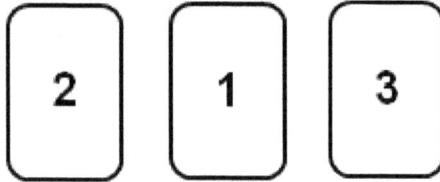

1: The present
2: The past
3: The future

1: Heart (emotions)/(fate)
2: Mind (thoughts)/(login)
3: Soul (instinct)/(outcome)

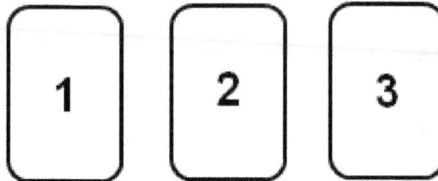

1: A week
2: A moon
3: A season

5 Card Spread

This spread should always be completed with a full deck.

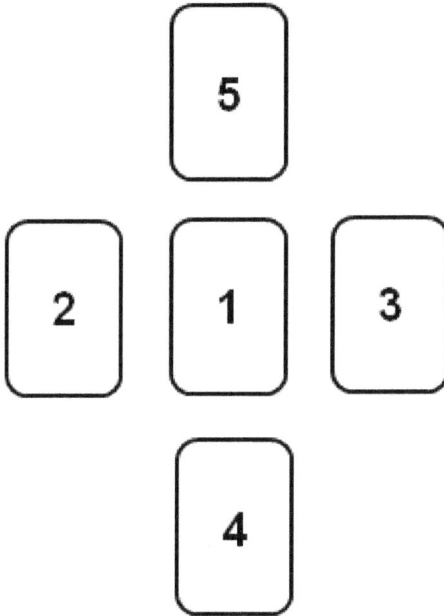

```
        ┌─────┐
        │     │
        │  5  │
        │     │
        └─────┘
┌─────┐ ┌─────┐ ┌─────┐
│     │ │     │ │     │
│  2  │ │  1  │ │  3  │
│     │ │     │ │     │
└─────┘ └─────┘ └─────┘
        ┌─────┐
        │     │
        │  4  │
        │     │
        └─────┘
```

1: The present
2: The past
3: The future
4: The reason
5: The outcome

Seven Card Spreads

The Horse Shoe spread uses the whole deck and is good for looking at any element of someone's life.

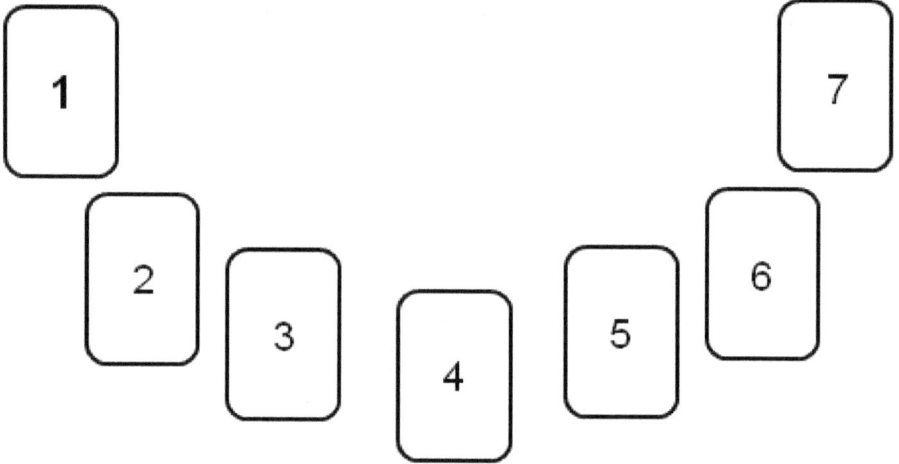

1   **7**

2

3

4

5

6

1: The past
2: The present
3: Immediate future
4: Advice on how to move forward
5: Other peoples opinions
6: Obstacles
7: Outcome

The Forked Road spread uses all the cards and is good for anyone facing a decision they are struggling to make.

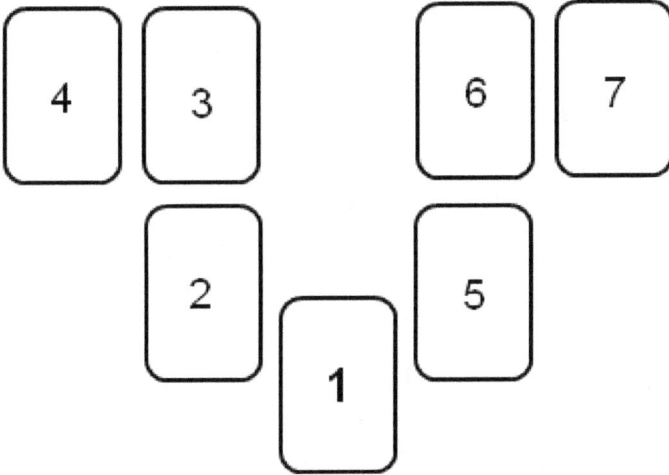

| 4 | 3 | | 6 | 7 |

| 2 | | 5 |

| 1 |

1: The present
2: Good points of 1st choice
3: Bad points of 1st choice
4: Outcome of 1st choice
5: Good points of 2nd choice
6: Bad points of 2nd choice
7: Outcome of 2nd choice

Thirteen Card Spread

The Wheel of the Year spread is good for looking at life in general, or a specific element of a persons life over a one year period.

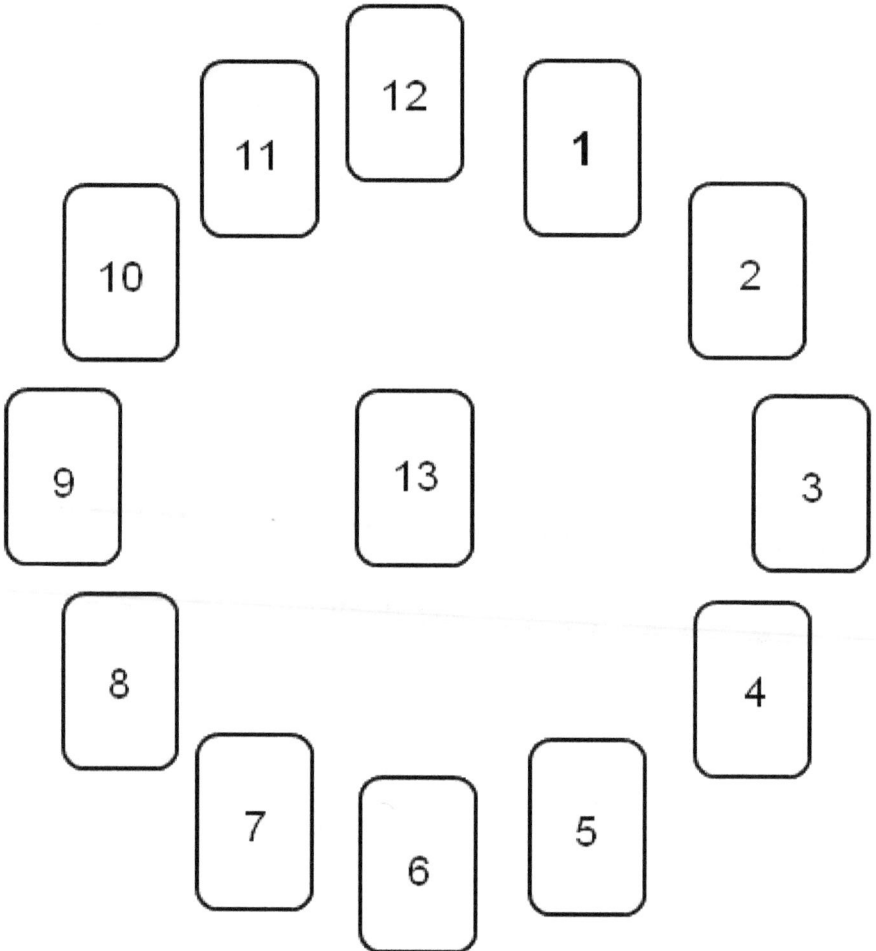

```
          12
     11         1
  10                2

 9        13          3

   8                4
      7    6    5
```

1-12: Each represent a month each, running in chronological order from the time that the reading is carried out.
13: This represents the general feel and prevailing theme of the year.

Giving Good Readings

My personal philosophy when giving readings to others it that they should be honest, but positive. I know of readers who will not read the inverted meaning of any card, as it often represents something negative. I believe doing this is a disservice to the person I am reading for, life does have negative elements, and the whole point of having a reading done is to be forewarned.

That said I strongly feel that a person should leave a tarot reading with a positive outlook on things. There are a few different ways in which you can do this, and still maintain your integrity as a reader:

1: Watch your language.
It's a fairly simply one. Be mindful of the way you explain the reading to people. If you are telling them something you think they will not be happy to hear, deliver the news gently.

2: Remind people that the future is not fixed.
So many people go into a reading with the misapprehension that what ever they are told is destined to happen no matter what. This of course is incorrect. The whole point of getting a reading is to learn what circumstance life may throw at you so that you can get more perspective and insight and choose how to deal with it better. Make sure people know that they can always choose which way to go in life.

3: Organic reading style.
If something comes up in a reading that makes someone unhappy, do a small side reading on it. Doing a quick 3 card spread asking "what positives can this person take from that" is a very good way to reassure people.

Example Readings

Spread: One Card Draw
Question: How should I deal with my developing career?
Card:

```
┌──────────┐
│          │
│   The    │
│  World   │
│          │
└──────────┘
```

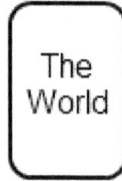

"The World" coming up as a result of this question is very positive, it means that the person has already had some success in their career, and has achieved some goals. It also means that the person should keep moving forward and developing, rather than getting cosy with what they've already got and failing to progress further.

Spread: The Forked Road
Question: Should we move house to a different area?
Cards:

Coins
8

Swords
4

Swords
8

Empress

3
Wands

Cups
4

8
Wands

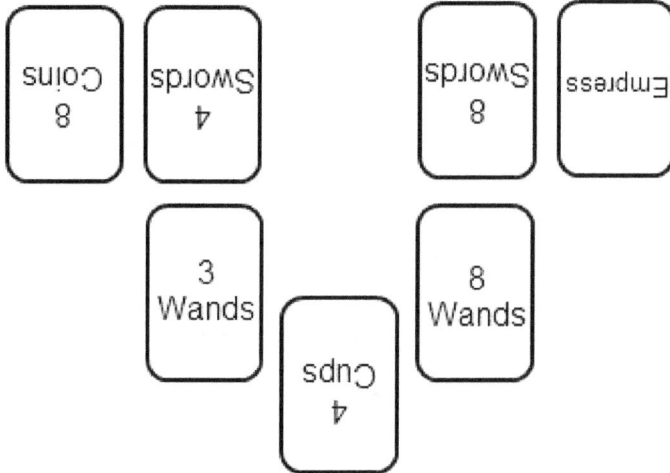

The 4 of cups coming up in the first position shows that the main driving force behind the considered house move is emotional unhappiness rather than practical reasons.

The three cards on the left were dealt whilst concentrating on the option of staying put. The 3 of Wands shows that despite feeling unhappy at the moment there has been happiness and success there, and there is more to come. The inverted 4 of Swords shows their may be a continued state of worry, though this seems to be based on the hypothetical. The inverted 8 of coins shows there may be some practical obstacles to overcome.

The three cards on the right were dealt whilst focusing on the option of moving. The 8 of Wands represents that a fresh start would add new energy to long term goals. The inverted 8 of Swords indicates that there would be disappointment after trying to bring visualised goals into being. The inverted Empress card indicates that moving could cause some serious issues in both work and domestic life.

Given that neither branch of this reading is particularly positive I decided to do the below side reading to see how the situation where they are currently living could be improved.

Spread: A Week, Moon & Season
Cards:

9 Wands	Queen Wands	5 Wands

The inverted 9 of Wands indicates that they need to make peace with things not working out and accept these things in order to move forward. The inverted Queen of Wands suggests that over the next month they should be wary of advice from others and trust their own judgement above all else. The 5 of wands shows that in a few months they will be able to better discuss and adapt to situations as they develop, and ultimately fell more settled.

I hope this little book has helped start you on a long path of development with the tarot, and wish you every success with all your divination endeavours.

Lily x